MW01038503

Appliqué Patterns

Donna Koepp

Copyright © 2012 Donna Koepp
All rights reserved.

ISBN-13: 978-1481239912

TABLE OF CONTENTS

HOMESPUN HOLIDAYS 12

ANGEL PATTERN 12
SNOWMAN APPLIQUE SHIRT 14
CHRISTMAS APPLIQUE SHIRT 16
POINSETTIA SWEATSHIRT PATTERN 18

BIRDS AND BIRDHOUSES 21

BIRDHOUSE TRIO SWEATSHIRT PATTERN 22
BIRD SWEATSHIRT JACKET..24
LACY BIRDHOUSE SWEATSHIRT PATTERN 26
HUMMINGBIRD SHIRT..28
CATS AND BIRDHOUSES SHIRT 30
BIRDHOUSE SWEATSHIRT PATTERN 32
YOYO BIRD APPLIQUE PATTERN 34
SUNFLOWER SHIRT...36

BUTTERFLY APPLIQUE 39

BUTTERFLY APPLIQUE SHIRT 40
BUTTERFLY HOUSE SHIRT..42

HEART PATTERNS 45

LOTS O' RED SHIRT 46
MAROON APPLIQUE SHIRT 48
HEARTS DENIM SHIRT 50
GROWING HEARTS T-SHIRT...52
HAVE A HEART PATTERN 54
HEARTS AND STARS SWEATSHIRT PATTERNS 56

CLOVER SHIRT 58

STAR APPLIQUE 61

LONE STAR VEST APPLIQUE PATTERN 62
STAR LIGHT STAR BRIGHT SHIRT...64
STAR LOG SHIRT 66
STARS & STRIPES T-SHIRT...68
SUNBURST SHIRT 70
QUILTER'S STAR PATTERN...72
COUNTRY STARS DENIM SHIRT 74
DANCING STARS JUMPER..76
HEARTS AND STARS SHIRT 78
PATCHWORK STAR 80
LONE STAR T-SHIRT..82
PANEL DENIM SHIRT...84

MISCELLANEOUS PATTERNS..87

ARKANSAS BLOCK SHIRT...88
ARROW APPLIQUE PATTERN..90
AUTUMN HARVEST SHIRT 92
BASKET PATCH SHIRT..94
CLOVER T-SHIRT 96
SOUTHWEST COYOTE PATTERN 98
DIAMONDS APPLIQUE SHIRT 100
FLAG T-SHIRT PATTERN 102
GOLDEN ROD SHIRT 104
HORSE SWEATSHIRT PATTERN 106
ICEBERG SWEATSHIRT PATTERN...108
PINK AND TEAL PATTERN 110
PINWHEEL SWEATSHIRT PATTERN...112
PREPPIE APPLIQUE PATTERN 114
SOUTHWESTERN HORSE PATTERN...116
TRIANGLE CARDIGAN JACKET 118
WINDMILL SWEATSHIRT PATTERN..120
WINDMILL VEST PATTERN 122

CHILDREN'S PATTERNS..125

CHILD'S CLOVER SWEATSHIRT 126
CHILD'S KITTY SWEATSHIRT 128
CHILD'S PUPPY SWEATSHIRT..130
CHILD'S TEDDY BEAR SWEATSHIRT...132

Appliqué Patterns

Introduction

Appliqué is a great way to add color and pizzazz to clothing, accessories and home décor items. It's easy to do, and with today's tools and materials, everyone can appliqué and turn out fresh and colorful projects in an afternoon.

Whether you sew or not, appliqué is fast, easy and adds a personal touch to your home and wardrobe. It's great for gifts and is simple enough that the kids can help, or even make their own creations.

The tools and materials are inexpensive, and there's a variety of ways to complete your projects. So, get out your scrap bag, scissors and iron, and start creating crafty keepsakes for yourself, your family and friends.

What Is Fusible Web?

Fusible web is a great product that can be used for hemming, repairs, crafting and, of course, appliqué. Created from a synthetic polymer that melts at a low temperature, it's a very thin layer of spun fibers that is available in rolls, sheets and tapes. When placed between two pieces of fabric, it bonds the layers together permanently with the application of heat.

It's available in a variety of weights produced by several manufacturers. You should use the weight that is similar to the fabric you are fusing. A heavier weight does not ensure a more permanent bond and can lead to problems if used incorrectly.

The kind of fusible web you'll use for appliqué projects come with a paper backing. Your pattern can be drawn directly on the paper, and the paper allows you to apply the web to the appliqué piece before fusing the two fabric layers together.

How To Appliqué With Fusible Transfer Web

With today's fusible transfer web, appliqué is a simple craft that anyone can easily learn. There's a number of brands and weights of fusible web available, so you should have no problem finding it at your local craft shop or fabric store.

As it becomes hard after it has been melted, heavy transfer web is not always a guarantee of a stronger bond. You should use the weight that is recommended by the manufacturer for the type of fabric you're using. To ensure your fabric fuses properly to the web, wash your cloth before using to remove any sizing.

First, choose your design. Besides the designs in this book, the internet is a wonderful place for royalty-free clip art you can download and print out. Another good source of designs is children's coloring books. These shapes are usually simple and perfect to use for appliqué.

Trace your shape on the paper side of the fusible transfer web, and place it on the wrong side of the fabric you'll be using to appliqué. Make sure the fabric is slightly larger than the fusible web so you don't inadvertently fuse the web to your ironing board.

Follow the manufacturer's instructions for temperature recommendations and ironing time.

Now that you've fused the web to the fabric, cut along the lines you've traced on the paper. Peel off the paper and position the appliqué on your garment. Follow the manufacturer's temperature recommendation and iron in place.

If the item is for a wall decoration and won't be laundered, that's all there is to it. If the appliqué is on an item of clothing or something that will get a lot of wear, you should stitch the edges. If you just want to prevent the edges from fraying, you can paint the cut edge with fabric paint or clear acrylic medium.

Hand Appliqué vs. Machine Appliqué

Now that you've gotten your appliqué adhered to your piece, you can either consider it complete, sew the border by hand or sew the edges with your sewing machine. Part of your decision is the end use of the item; personal preference and the degree of complexity are other factors.

If you want a handcrafted, homey look to your piece, hand stitching the edges of your appliqué is a good option. You can use a variety of threads and yarns like wool or acrylic crewel yarn, embroidery floss or metallic threads. Unusual fibers like raffia or twine give an interesting and unique look.

You can use a simple blanket stitch, or you can get fancy with embroidery stitches such as a chain stitch, cross stitch, fly stitch or lazy daisy stitch. Use different stitches for different areas of the appliqué pieces and contrasting colors to add texture and pizzazz.

If you use your sewing machine to edge your appliqué, you'll probably use a zigzag or satin stitch. A zigzag stitch will take less time, but it won't conceal the edges. A satin stitch will conceal the appliqué edges and make the item far more durable. You can vary the width of the satin stitch or zigzag stitch, and a variety of widths and thread colors will add interest to the piece.

What Can I Appliqué?

If it's cloth, cute and could use a little extra zing, it's a potential for the appliqué fairy! You can appliqué almost anything. It just depends on what fabrics you select for your appliqué and the method you use to attach your pieces.

If you're planning to appliqué new clothing, wash the garment. This will pre-shrink the item and remove any sizing that may interfere with the fusible web bonding process. Your appliqué material should be pre-washed as well.

If the item is not washable, such as a home décor item, be especially careful that the fusible web bonds securely. Delicate items require extra care, as the heat of the iron may damage them. For this type of item, use the minimum heat setting required to fuse the fabric, and use a pressing cloth to protect the fibers.

You can add appliqué to pillows, purses and tote bags, jackets, scarves and table linens. Customize guest towels, kitchen accessories or even curtains and pet products. Once you start, you'll find appliqué opportunities everywhere!

DONNA KOEPP

Everyone loves to decorate for Christmas. Decorate yourself as well as your home with fun and fanciful appliqués for shirts, sweatshirts, pillows, towels and children's items.

Angels, snowmen and poinsettias add a special holiday look that everyone will enjoy. Use specialty Christmas fabrics, or use up some of the scraps in your stash to create festive outfits and accessories to dress up yourself and your home for the holidays.

HOMESPUN HOLIDAYS

Angel Pattern

If we were all a little more like Angels, earth would be a little more like heaven. You will be a hit in this angelic design - sew it on a denim shirt or jumper. Angel pattern can also be used on a jacket or pillow.

Print the full size Angel Pattern:

www.FreeApplique.com/Patterns/angelpat1.html
www.FreeApplique.com/Patterns/angelpat2.html

Supplies:

Denim shirt
Small amounts of fabric
Thread to match the fabric
Two small buttons
Fusible web

Angel Shirt Instructions

Follow the fusible web manufacturer's iron on instructions and iron the fusible web on the wrong side of the fabric.

From the fabric with the fusible web applied, cut a piece 17 1/2" by 1 1/4" wide. This will be the collar piece.

Trace the pattern pieces on the fusible web paper backing and cut out all pieces. Peel the fusible web paper backing from all pieces. Position each piece on shirt with right side of the fabric up. Iron pattern pieces on the shirt as directed for the fusible web.

Sew pieces on with a medium tight zigzag stitch. You need to sew a small tight zigzag stitch from each of the three small stars to her hand.

When you are done, sew the two small buttons on the angel's dress. Use a black fabric marker pen to make eyes on the angel's face.

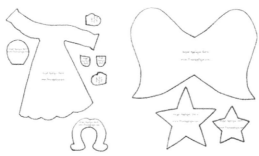

Snowman Applique Shirt

Here is a quick and easy project that will add a touch of winter to any denim shirt. The applique would also look nice on a Christmas stocking.

Print the full size Applique Pattern:
www.freeapplique.com/applique.data/snowman1.jpg

Supplies:

Denim shirt
Fabric scraps
Thread to match
Fusible web

Snowman Applique Shirt Instructions

Follow the fusible web manufacturer's iron on instructions
and iron the fusible web on the wrong side of the fabric.

From the fabric with the fusible web applied, cut two pieces
17 1/2" long by 1 1/4" wide. One will be for the collar and the
other one will be used on a long sleeve shirt on the cuffs.

Trace the pattern pieces on the fusible web paper backing
and cut out all pieces. Peel the fusible web paper backing
from all pieces. Position each piece on shirt with right side of
the fabric up. Iron pattern pieces on the shirt as directed for
the fusible web.

Sew pieces on with a medium tight zigzag stitch.

Christmas Applique Shirt

Behind every seamstress is a huge pile of fabric.

Print the full size applique patterns:
www.FreeApplique.com/applique.data/2snowmen1.jpg
www.FreeApplique.com/applique.data/2snowmen2.jpg

Supplies:

Denim shirt
Fabric scraps
Thread to match
Fusible web

Christmas Applique Shirt Instructions

Follow the fusible web manufacturer's iron on instructions
and iron the fusible web on the wrong side of the fabric.

From the fabric with the fusible web applied, cut two pieces
17 1/2" long by 1 1/4" wide. One will be for the collar and the
other one will be used on a long sleeve shirt on the cuffs.

Trace the pattern pieces on the fusible web paper backing
and cut out all pieces. Peel the fusible web paper backing
from all pieces. Position each piece on shirt with right side of
the fabric up. Iron pattern pieces on the shirt as directed for
the fusible web.

Sew pieces on with a medium tight zigzag stitch.

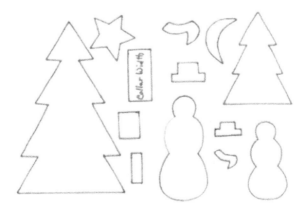

Poinsettia Sweatshirt Pattern

Friends are like fabric,
You can never have enough!

Print the full size applique patterns:
www.FreeApplique.com/applique.data/poinsettapattern.gif

Supplies:

Sweatshirt
Fabric scraps
Thread to match fabric
Fusible web

Poinsettia Christmas Sweatshirt Instructions

Follow the fusible web manufacturer's iron on instructions and iron the fusible web on the wrong side of the fabric.

Trace the pattern pieces on the fusible web paper backing and cut out all pieces. Peel the fusible web paper backing from all pieces. Position each piece on sweatshirt. Iron pattern pieces on the sweatshirt as directed for the fusible web.

Sew the pattern pieces on with a medium zigzag stitch.

Applique

Birds
and
Birdhouses

BIRDS AND BIRDHOUSES

Birdhouse patterns are charming and whimsical additions that add color and texture. You can use just about any fabric to create your multi-colored birdhouse, and they're a great way to use up scraps.

Don't limit your palette to just a couple of fabrics. Use solids, prints, florals and stripes to create fanciful birdhouses that brighten up a plain shirt or add color and pattern to home decorating items.

Birdhouse Trio Sweatshirt Pattern

My husband lets me buy all the fabric I can hide.

Print the full size applique patterns:

www.FreeApplique.com/applique.data/fencess1.jpg
www.FreeApplique.com/applique.data/fencess2.jpg

Supplies:

Sweatshirt
Fabric scraps
Thread to match fabric
Fusible web

Birdhouse Trio Sweatshirt Instructions

Follow the fusible web manufacturer's iron on instructions and iron the fusible web on the wrong side of the fabric.

Trace the pattern pieces on the fusible web paper backing and cut out all pieces. Peel the fusible web paper backing from all pieces. Position each piece on sweatshirt. Iron pattern pieces on the sweatshirt as directed for the fusible web. Sew the pattern pieces on with a medium zigzag stitch.

Bird Sweatshirt Jacket

I got a sewing machine for my husband. Good trade, eh?

This birdhouse scene sewing machine applique pattern would be stunning on a sweatshirt jacket, denim shirt or wall quilt.

Print the full size applique patterns:

www.FreeApplique.com/Patterns/birdjacketpat1.html
www.FreeApplique.com/Patterns/birdjacketpat2.html

Supplies:

Sweatshirt jacket
Fabric scraps
5 buttons
Thread to match fabric
Fusible web

Bird Sweatshirt Jacket Instructions

This design is on a sweatshirt jacket but can be put on a plain sweatshirt or a denim shirt as well.

Follow the fusible web manufacturer's iron on instructions and iron the fusible web on the wrong side of the fabric.

Trace the pattern pieces on the fusible web paper backing with a pencil and cut out all pieces. Position each piece on sweatshirt jacket with right side of the fabric up.

Iron pattern pieces on the sweatshirt as directed for the fusible web.

Sew the pattern pieces on with a medium zigzag stitch. Now sew some buttons on the birdhouses.

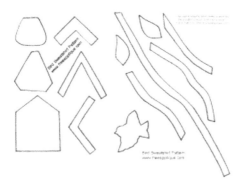

Lacy Birdhouse Sweatshirt Pattern

When life hands you scraps, applique a shirt!

Print the full size applique patterns:
www.FreeApplique.com/applique.data/laceyss1.jpg
www.FreeApplique.com/applique.data/laceyss2.jpg

Supplies:

Sweatshirt
Fabric scraps
Thread to match fabric
Fusible web
Scraps of Lace

Lacy Birdhouse Sweatshirt Instructions

Follow the fusible web manufacturer's iron on instructions and iron the fusible web on the wrong side of the fabric.

Trace the pattern pieces on the fusible web paper backing and cut out all pieces. Peel the fusible web paper backing from all pieces. Position each piece on sweatshirt. Iron pattern pieces on the sweatshirt as directed for the fusible web. Sew the pattern pieces on with a medium zigzag stitch.

After sewing everything onto the sweatshirt, measure scraps of lace to put on the roof and sew them to the sweatshirt. The lace should be wide enough to cover just the roof of the birdhouses.

Hummingbird Shirt

I'd rather be stitchin' than in the kitchen.

Print the full size applique patterns:
www.FreeApplique.com/Patterns/hummingbirdpat.html

Supplies:

Denim shirt
Fabric scraps
Thread to match
Fusible web

Hummingbird Shirt Instructions

Follow the fusible web manufacturer's iron on instructions and iron the fusible web on the wrong side of the fabric.

From the fabric with the fusible web applied, cut two pieces 17 1/2" long by 1 1/4" wide. One will be for the collar and the other one will be used on a long sleeve shirt on the cuffs.

Trace the pattern pieces on the fusible web paper backing and cut out all pieces. Peel the fusible web paper backing from all pieces. Position each piece on shirt with right side of the fabric up. Iron pattern pieces on the shirt as directed for the fusible web.

Sew pieces on with a medium tight zigzag stitch.

Cats and Birdhouses Shirt

Sew much fabric....sew little time.

Print the full size applique patterns:
www.FreeApplique.com/Patterns/catbirdpat1.html
www.FreeApplique.com/Patterns/catbirdpat2.html
www.FreeApplique.com/Patterns/catbirdpat3.html

Supplies:

Denim shirt
Fabric scraps
Thread to match
Fusible web

Cats and Birdhouses Shirt Instructions

Follow the fusible web manufacturer's iron on instructions
and iron the fusible web on the wrong side of the fabric.

From the fabric with the fusible web applied, cut one piece
17 1/2" long by 1 1/4" wide. This piece will be used on the
collar.

Trace the pattern pieces on the fusible web paper backing
and cut out all pieces. Peel the fusible web paper backing
from all pieces. Position each piece on shirt with right side of
the fabric up. Iron pattern pieces on the shirt as directed for
the fusible web.

Sew pieces on with a medium tight zigzag stitch.

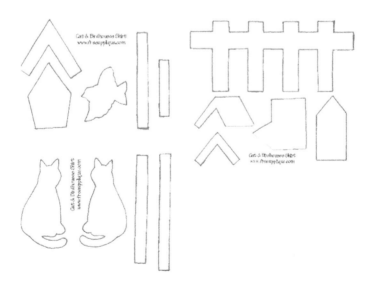

Birdhouse Sweatshirt Pattern

Add a homespun touch to any sweatshirt. The birdhouse pattern would also be great to use for applique on quilts.

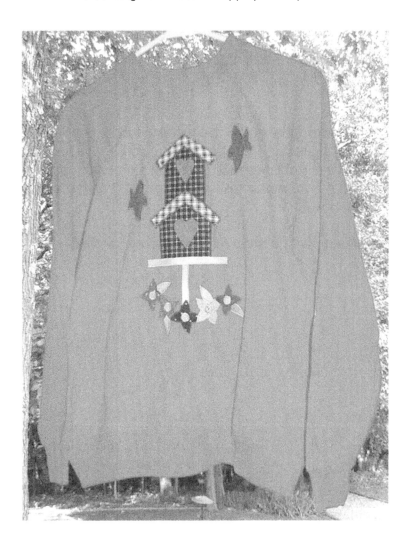

Print the full size applique patterns:
www.FreeApplique.com/applique.data/redss1aa.jpg
www.FreeApplique.com/applique.data/redss2aa.jpg

Supplies:

Sweatshirt
Fabric scraps
Thread to match fabric
Fusible web

Birdhouse Sweatshirt Instructions

Follow the fusible web manufacturer's iron on instructions and iron the fusible web on the wrong side of the fabric.

Trace the pattern pieces on the fusible web paper backing and cut out all pieces. Peel the fusible web paper backing from all pieces. Position each piece on sweatshirt. Iron pattern pieces on the sweatshirt as directed for the fusible web.

Sew the pattern pieces on with a medium zigzag stitch.

YoYo Bird Applique Pattern

Any day spent sewing is a good day.

Sew this free birdhouse applique quilt pattern on a shirt or wall quilt. Cute birdhouse pattern uses yoyos for flowers.

Print the full size applique patterns:
www.FreeApplique.com/Patterns/birdpat1aa.html
www.FreeApplique.com/Patterns/birdpat2aa.html
www.FreeApplique.com/Patterns/birdpat3aa.html
www.FreeApplique.com/Patterns/birdpat4aa.html

Supplies:

Denim shirt
Fabric scraps
Thread to match fabric
4 large buttons
4 medium buttons
Fusible web

YoYo Birdhouse Instructions

Follow the fusible web manufacturer's iron on instructions and iron the fusible web on the wrong side of the fabric.

From the fabric with the fusible web applied, cut a piece 17 1/2" long and 1 1/4" wide. This will be the collar piece.

Trace the pattern pieces on the fusible web paper backing and cut out all pieces. Peel the fusible web paper backing from all pieces. Position each piece on shirt with the right side up. Iron patterns on as directed for the fusible web.

Sew pieces on with a medium width, tight zigzag stitch. Sew buttons on the birdhouse.

To make yoyo's, fold the edges 1/4" and run a gathering stitch along edge. Pull thread to make a yoyo and knot thread on bottom of yoyo. Sew yoyos on the shirt with a medium button in the center.

Sunflower Shirt

Friendships are sewn one stitch at a time.

Print the full size applique patterns:
www.FreeApplique.com/applique.data/sunflower1aa.gif
www.FreeApplique.com/applique.data/sunflower2aa.gif

Supplies:

Denim Shirt
Fabric scraps
Fusible web
Thread to match fabric

Sunflower Shirt Instructions

Follow the fusible web manufacturer's iron on instructions and iron the fusible web on the wrong side of the fabric.

From the fabric with the fusible web applied, cut a piece 17 1/2" long and 1 1/4" wide. This will be the collar piece.

Trace the pattern pieces on the fusible web paper backing and cut out all pieces. Peel the fusible web paper backing from all pieces. Position each piece on shirt with right side of the fabric up. Iron patterns on as directed for the fusible web.

Sew pieces on with a medium width tight zigzag stitch.

BUTTERFLY APPLIQUE

Add all the colors of the rainbow with fanciful butterflies. Embellish a shirt, skirt or a pair of little girl's pants with fluttering butterflies. Butterflies are great for adding color and pattern and can be a creative starting point for a decorating theme in a little girl's bedroom or a guest bathroom.

Use delicate florals and bold solid fabrics to create a combination that's eye-catching and colorful. Small or large, these appliqués can be applied as an overall design or as a single embellishment on a small item like a hat or finger towel.

Butterfly Applique Shirt

Ready...Set...Sew!

Print the full size applique patterns:

www.FreeApplique.com/Patterns/butterflypat1.html
www.FreeApplique.com/Patterns/butterflypat2.html

Supplies:
Denim shirt
Fabric scraps
Thread to match fabric
Fusible web

Butterfly Shirt Instructions

Follow the fusible web manufacturer's iron on instructions and iron the fusible web on the wrong side of the fabric.

From the fabric with the fusible web applied, cut a piece 17 1/2" long by 1 1/4" wide. This will be the collar piece.

Trace the pattern pieces on the fusible web paper backing and cut out all pieces. Peel the fusible web paper backing from all pieces. Position each piece on shirt with right side of the fabric up. Iron patterns on as directed for the fusible web.

Sew pieces on with a medium width tight zigzag stitch.

When you are done sewing the pieces on, you are ready to start making the body and antennas on the butterflies and also the holes for the butterfly house.

For the butterfly house, you will need black thread and the largest width on your machine with a tight zigzag stitch.

For the bodies of the butterflies, use a large tight zigzag stitch and for the antennas use a very small tight zigzag stitch.

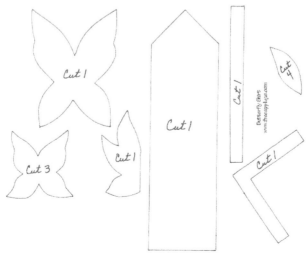

Butterfly House Shirt

Print the full size applique patterns:
www.FreeApplique.com/applique.data/butterss1.jpg

Supplies:

Denim shirt
Fabric scraps
Thread to match fabric
Fusible web

Butterfly House Shirt Instructions

Follow the fusible web manufacturer's iron on instructions and iron the fusible web on the wrong side of the fabric.

Trace the pattern pieces on the fusible web paper backing and cut out all the pieces. Peel the fusible web paper backing from all pieces. Position each piece on shirt with right side of the fabric up. Iron patterns on as directed for the fusible web.

Sew pieces on with a medium width tight zigzag stitch.

When you are done sewing the pieces on the sweatshirt, you are ready to start making the body and antennas on the butterflies.

For the butterfly house, you will need black thread and the largest width on your machine with a tight zigzag.

For the bodies of the butterfly, you will need a large tight zigzag and for the antenna's you will need a very small tight zigzag stitch.

Heart Applique

HEART PATTERNS

You don't need to wait for Valentine's Day to start sewing hearts. Hearts are one of the most popular decorating themes for home and apparel, so you know you won't miss the mark when you appliqué hearts.

Funky, traditional, contemporary or eclectic, hearts of all shapes and sizes are great to add on gifts, clothing for everyone and accessories for the home. Let your imagination and scrap bin run wild with all the colors and patterns.

Lots o' Red Shirt

She who dies with the most fabric.....wins.

Print the full size applique patterns:
www.FreeApplique.com/applique.data/redstar1a.gif
www.FreeApplique.com/applique.data/redstar2a.gif

Supplies:

Denim Shirt
Fabric scraps
Thread to match fabric
Fusible web

Lots O' Red Shirt Instructions

Follow the fusible web manufacturer's iron on instructions and iron the fusible web on the wrong side of the fabric.

From the fabric with the fusible web applied, cut a piece 17 1/2" long by 1 1/4" wide. This will be the collar piece.

Trace the pattern pieces on the fusible web paper backing and cut out all pieces. Peel the fusible web paper backing from all pieces. Position each piece on shirt with right side of the fabric up. Iron pattern pieces on the shirt as directed for the fusible web.

Sew pieces on with a tight zigzag stitch.

Maroon Applique Shirt

If I stitch fast enough does it count as an aerobic exercise?

Print the full size applique patterns:

www.FreeApplique.com/applique.data/maroon1.gif
www.FreeApplique.com/applique.data/maroon2.gif

Supplies:

Maroon shirt or a denim shirt
Fabric scraps
Thread to match fabric
Fusible web

Maroon Applique Shirt Instructions

Follow the fusible web manufacturer's iron on instructions and iron the fusible web on the wrong side of the fabric.

From the fabric with the fusible web applied, cut two pieces 17 1/2" long by 1 1/4" wide. One will be for the collar and the other one will be used on the cuffs of the long sleeve shirt.

Trace the pattern pieces on the fusible web paper backing and cut out all pieces. Peel the fusible web paper backing from all pieces. Position each piece on the shirt with the right side of the fabric up. Iron the pattern pieces on the shirt as directed for the fusible web.

Sew pieces on with a medium tight zigzag stitch.

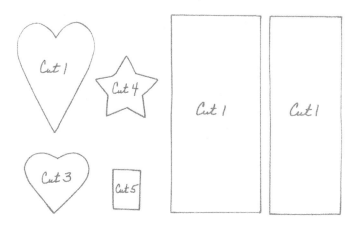

Hearts Denim Shirt

Itchin' to be Stitchin'.

Print the full size applique patterns:

www.FreeApplique.com/applique.data/grow1.gif
www.FreeApplique.com/applique.data/grow3.gif
www.FreeApplique.com/applique.data/grow2.gif

Supplies:

Denim Shirt
Fabric scraps
Thread to match fabric
Four medium buttons
21" of jute for bows
Fusible web

Growing Hearts Denim Shirt Instructions

Follow the fusible web manufacturer's iron on instructions and iron the fusible web on the wrong side of the fabric.

From the fabric with the fusible web applied, cut a piece 17 1/2" long and 1 1/4" wide. This will be the collar piece.

Trace the pattern pieces on the fusible web paper backing and cut out all pieces. Peel the fusible web paper backing from all pieces. Position each piece on shirt with right side of the fabric up. Iron patterns on as directed for the fusible web.

Sew pieces on with a medium width tight zigzag stitch.

Make three bows out of the jute. These go near the top of the three hearts on the right side of the shirt. Place a button on top of the jute bow and hand sew them both in place. Hand sew the other button on the large heart on the other side of the shirt.

This shirt looks nice with the Growing Hearts T-Shirt underneath.

Growing Hearts T-Shirt

When I learned how to sew...I forgot how to cook.

Print the full size applique patterns:
www.FreeApplique.com/applique.data/gh1.gif
www.FreeApplique.com/applique.data/gh4.gif
www.FreeApplique.com/applique.data/gh3.gif
www.FreeApplique.com/applique.data/gh2.gif

Supplies:

One T-Shirt
Fabric scraps
Thread to match fabric
Three medium buttons
21" of Jute for bows
Fusible web

Growing Hearts T-shirt Instructions

Follow the fusible web manufacturer's iron on instructions and iron the fusible web on the wrong side of the fabric.

Trace the pattern pieces on the fusible web paper backing and cut out all pieces. Remove fusible web from all pieces. Position each piece on T-shirt with right side of the pattern pieces up. Iron pattern pieces on as directed for the fusible web.

Sew pieces on with a medium width loose zigzag stitch.

Using jute, make three bows. These go on the hearts down the front of the T-shirt. Place a button on top of the jute bow and hand sew both in place.

Have a Heart Pattern

Print the full size applique patterns:
www.FreeApplique.com/applique.data/haveaheartpatt.jpg

Supplies:

Sweatshirt
Fabric scraps
Thread to match fabric
Fusible web
Purchased knit collar

Have a Heart Sweatshirt Instructions

Follow the fusible web manufacturer's iron on instructions and iron the fusible web on the wrong side of the fabric.

Trace the pattern pieces on the fusible web paper backing and cut out all pieces. Peel the fusible web paper backing from all pieces. Position each piece on the sweatshirt. Iron the pattern pieces on the sweatshirt as in the directions for the fusible web.

Sew the pattern pieces on with a medium zigzag stitch.

Hearts and Stars Sweatshirt Patterns

Will work for fabric!

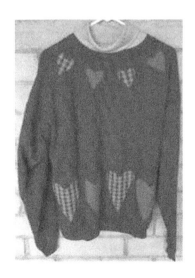

Hearts and Stars Sweatshirts Pattern

Print the full size applique patterns:
www.FreeApplique.com/applique.data/starss.gif
www.FreeApplique.com/applique.data/heartss.gif

Supplies:

Sweatshirt
Fabric scraps
Thread to match fabric
Fusible web

Hearts and Stars Instructions

Follow the fusible web manufacturer's iron on instructions
and iron the fusible web on the wrong side of the fabric.

Trace the pattern pieces on the fusible web paper backing
and cut out all pieces. Peel the fusible web paper backing
from all pieces. Position each piece on sweatshirt. Iron
pattern pieces on the sweatshirt as directed for the fusible
web.

Sew the pattern pieces on with a medium zigzag stitch. I
have put the same pattern on the back of the sweatshirt that
is on the front.

Clover Shirt

One yard of fabric, like one cookie, is never enough.
You'll be a star in this denim shirt.

Print the full size applique patterns:
www.FreeApplique.com/applique.data/clovershirtpattern2.jpg

Supplies:

Denim shirt
Fabric scraps
Thread to match
Fusible web

Clover Shirt Instructions

Follow the fusible web manufacturer's iron on instructions and iron the fusible web on the wrong side of the fabric.

From the fabric with the fusible web applied, cut two pieces 17 1/2" long by 1 1/4" wide. One will be for the collar and the other one will be used on a long sleeve shirt on the cuffs.

Trace the pattern pieces on the fusible web paper backing and cut out all pieces. Peel the fusible web paper backing from all pieces. Position each piece on shirt with right side of the fabric up. Iron pattern pieces on the shirt as directed for the fusible web.

Sew pieces on with a medium tight zigzag stitch.

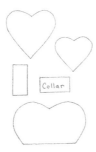

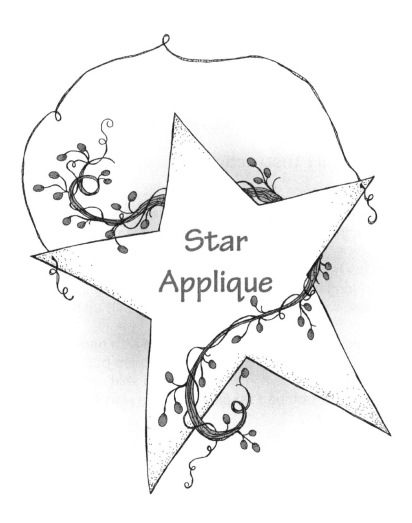

Star Applique

STAR APPLIQUE

You don't need to be patriotic to use stars. Star appliqués are a natural to add Independence Day fun to your summer home decorations, but don't stop there. Create colorful shirts and aprons, or decorate a set of picnic napkins with bright and spirited stars.

If you're a quilting fan, star quilting patterns make perfect appliqués to add to a sweatshirt or jacket. Add a Texas Star or patchwork star to a jumper for yourself or your favorite little one. Use small stars, along with hearts and other designs, to create a one-of-a-kind tote bag that will gather loads of compliments.

Lone Star Vest Applique Pattern

Buttons and patches and the cold wind blowing
...the days pass quickly when I am sewing.

Print the full size applique patterns:

www.FreeApplique.com/applique.data/vest1.gif
www.FreeApplique.com/applique.data/vest2.gif

Supplies:

Vest
Fabric scraps

Thread to match fabric
Fusible web
Six small buttons

Lone Star Vest Instructions

Follow the fusible web manufacturer's iron on instructions and iron the fusible web on the wrong side of the fabric.

From the fabric with the fusible web applied, cut a piece 17 1/2" by 1 1/4" wide. This will be the collar piece.

Trace the pattern pieces on the fusible web paper backing and cut out all pieces. Remove fusible web from all pieces. Position each piece on vest with right side of the fabric up. Iron pattern pieces on as directed for the fusible web. Sew pieces on with a medium width tight zigzag stitch.

Sew buttons on all four corners of the large square. Sew a button on the other side of the shirt in each of the triangles.

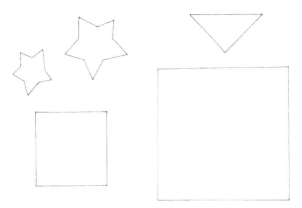

Star Light Star Bright Shirt

I'd rather be stitchin' than in the kitchen.

Print the full size applique patterns:
www.FreeApplique.com/applique.data/starlight1.gif
www.FreeApplique.com/applique.data/starlight2.gif
www.FreeApplique.com/applique.data/starlight3.gif

Supplies:

Denim shirt
Fabric scraps
Thread to match
Fusible web

Star Light Star Bright Shirt Instructions

Follow the fusible web manufacturer's iron on instructions
and iron the fusible web on the wrong side of the fabric.

From the fabric with the fusible web applied, cut two pieces
17 1/2" long by 1 1/4" wide. One will be for the collar and the
other one will be used on a long sleeve shirt on the cuffs.

Trace the pattern pieces on the fusible web paper backing
and cut out all pieces. Peel the fusible web paper backing
from all pieces. Position each piece on shirt with right side of
the fabric up. Iron pattern pieces on the shirt as directed for
the fusible web.

Sew pieces on with a medium tight zigzag stitch.

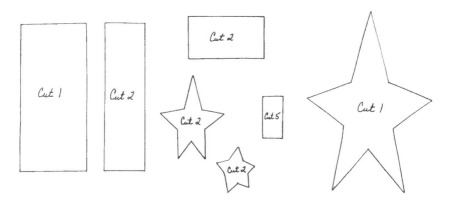

Star Log Shirt

A family stitched together with love, seldom unravels.

Print the full size applique patterns:
http://www.freeapplique.com/applique.data/starshirt1.gif
http://www.freeapplique.com/applique.data/starshirt2.gif

Supplies:

Denim shirt
Fabric scraps
Thread to match fabric
Six small buttons
Fusible web

Star Log Shirt Instructions

Follow the fusible web manufacturer's iron on instructions and iron the fusible web on the wrong side of the fabric.

From the fabric with the fusible web applied, cut a piece 17 1/2" long and 1 1/4" wide. This will be the collar piece.

Trace the pattern pieces on the fusible web paper backing and cut out all pieces. Peel the fusible web paper backing from all pieces. Position each piece on shirt with right side of the fabric up. Iron patterns on as directed for the fusible web.

Sew pieces on with a medium width tight zigzag stitch.

Sew a button on each of the large rectangles on top. Sew a button on two of the smaller rectangles on top.

Stars & Stripes T-Shirt

I was Cut out to be RICH, but I was Sewed up WRONG.

Stitch up this quick and easy T-shirt. This T-shirt looks great under the Star Log Denim shirt.

Print the full size applique patterns:

www.FreeApplique.com/applique.data/StarT1.gif
www.FreeApplique.com/applique.data/starT2.gif

Supplies:

T-Shirt
Fabric scraps
Thread to match fabric
Four small buttons
Fusible web

Stars & Stripes T-Shirt Instructions

Follow the fusible web manufacturer's iron on instructions and iron the fusible web on the wrong side of the fabric.

Trace the pattern pieces on the fusible web paper backing and cut out all pieces. Peel the fusible web paper backing from all pieces. Position each piece on shirt with right side of the fabric up. Iron patterns on as directed for the fusible web.

Sew pieces on with a medium width loose zigzag stitch.

Sew a button on the top of each large rectangles.

Sunburst Shirt

I'd rather be stitchin than in the kitchen.

Print the full size applique patterns:
www.FreeApplique.com/Patterns/sunburstpat1.html
www.FreeApplique.com/Patterns/sunburstpat2.html

Supplies:

Denim shirt
Fabric scraps
Thread to match
Fusible web

Sunburst Shirt

Follow the fusible web manufacturer's iron on instructions
and iron the fusible web on the wrong side of the fabric.

From the fabric with the fusible web applied, cut two pieces
17 1/2" long by 1 1/4" wide. One will be for the collar and the
other one will be used on a long sleeve shirt on the cuffs.

Trace the pattern pieces on the fusible web paper backing
and cut out all pieces. Peel the fusible web paper backing
from all pieces. Position each piece on shirt with right side of
the fabric up. Iron pattern pieces on the shirt as directed for
the fusible web. Sew pieces on with a medium tight zigzag
stitch.

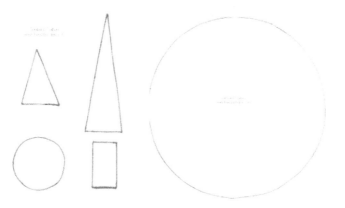

Quilter's Star Pattern

Print the full size applique patterns:
www.FreeApplique.com/applique.data/quilterspattern.jpg

Supplies:

Sweatshirt
Fabric scraps
Thread to match fabric
Fusible web

Quilter's Star Sweatshirt Instructions

Follow the fusible web manufacturer's iron on instructions and iron the fusible web on the wrong side of the fabric.

Trace the pattern pieces on the fusible web paper backing and cut out all pieces. Peel the fusible web paper backing from all pieces. Position each piece on sweatshirt. Iron pattern pieces on the sweatshirt as directed for the fusible web.

Sew the pattern pieces on with a medium zigzag stitch.

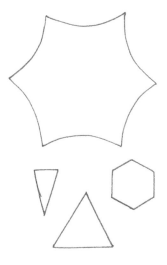

Country Stars Denim Shirt

Memories are stitched with love.
Sew this free applique pattern on a denim shirt, vest, or quilt.

Print the full size applique patterns:

www.FreeApplique.com/applique.data/countrystars1.jpg
www.FreeApplique.com/applique.data/countrystars2.jpg

Supplies:

Denim shirt
Fabric scraps
Thread to match fabric
Fusible web
Six small buttons

Country Stars Shirt Instructions

Follow the fusible web manufacturer's iron on instructions
and iron the fusible web on the wrong side of the fabric.

From the fabric with the fusible web applied, cut a piece 17
1/2" long and 1 1/4" wide. This will be the collar piece.

Trace the pattern pieces on the fusible web paper backing
and cut out all pieces. Remove fusible web from all pieces.
Position each piece on shirt with right side of the fabric up.
Iron pattern pieces on as directed for the fusible web. Sew
pieces on with a medium width tight zigzag stitch. Or you
can vary the stitch from tight to loose on different parts of the
pattern pieces.

Sew buttons on all four corners of the large square. Sew a
button on the other side of the shirt in each of the triangles.

You can mix and match different pieces of fabric.

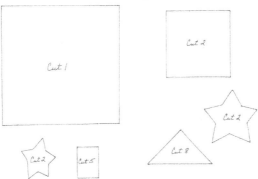

Dancing Stars Jumper

A penny saved is a penny to spend on fabric.

Print the full size applique patterns:
www.FreeApplique.com/applique.data/starpatt.jpg
www.FreeApplique.com/applique.data/hankiepatt1.jpg
www.FreeApplique.com/applique.data/hankiepatt2.jpg

Supplies:

Denim shirt
Fabric scraps
Thread to match
Fusible web

Dancing Stars Jumper Instructions

Follow the fusible web manufacturer's iron on instructions
and iron the fusible web on the wrong side of the fabric.

From the fabric with the fusible web applied, cut two pieces
17 1/2" long by 1 1/4" wide. One will be for the collar and the
other one will be used on a long sleeve shirt on the cuffs.

Trace the pattern pieces on the fusible web paper backing
and cut out all pieces. Peel the fusible web paper backing
from all pieces. Position each piece on shirt with right side of
the fabric up. Iron pattern pieces on the shirt as directed for
the fusible web.

Sew pieces on with a medium tight zigzag stitch.

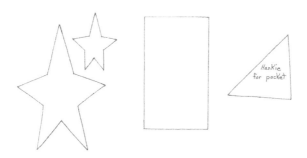

Hearts and Stars Shirt

Old seamstresses never go crazy, they just stay on pins and needles.

Print the full size applique patterns:
www.FreeApplique.com/applique.data/hstar1a.jpg
www.FreeApplique.com/applique.data/hstar2a.jpg

Supplies:

Denim shirt
Fabric scraps
Thread to match fabric
Fusible web

Hearts and Stars Shirt Instructions

Follow the fusible web manufacturer's iron on instructions and iron the fusible web on the wrong side of the fabric.

From the fabric with the fusible web applied, cut two pieces 17 1/2" long by 1 1/4" wide. One will be for the collar and the other one will be used on a long sleeve shirt on the cuffs.

Trace the pattern pieces on the fusible web paper backing and cut out all pieces. Peel the fusible web paper backing from all pieces. Position each piece on shirt with right side of the fabric up. Iron pattern pieces on the shirt as directed for the fusible web.

Sew pieces on with a medium tight zigzag stitch.

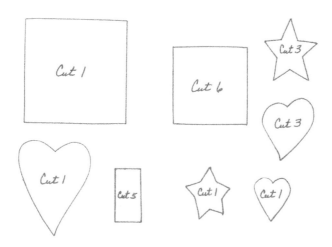

Patchwork Star

One yard of fabric, like one cookie, is never enough.

Print the full size applique patterns:
www.FreeApplique.com/applique.data/triangle.jpg

Supplies:

Denim shirt
Fabric scraps
Thread to match
Fusible web

Patchwork Star Shirt Instructions

Follow the fusible web manufacturer's iron on instructions and iron the fusible web on the wrong side of the fabric.

From the fabric with the fusible web applied, cut two pieces 17 1/2" long by 1 1/4" wide. One will be for the collar and the other one will be used on a long sleeve shirt on the cuffs.

Trace the pattern pieces on the fusible web paper backing and cut out all pieces. Peel the fusible web paper backing from all pieces. Position each piece on shirt with right side of the fabric up. Iron pattern pieces on the shirt as directed for the fusible web.

Sew pieces on with a medium tight zigzag stitch.

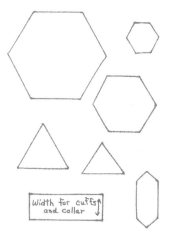

Lone Star T-Shirt

I was Cut out to be RICH, but I was Sewed up WRONG.

Print the full size applique patterns:
www.FreeApplique.com/applique.data/lonestar1.gif
www.FreeApplique.com/applique.data/lonestar2.gif

Supplies:

T-Shirt
Fabric scraps
Thread to match fabric
Four small buttons
Fusible web

Lone Star T-Shirt Instructions

Follow the fusible web manufacturer's iron on instructions
and iron the fusible web on the wrong side of the fabric.

Trace the pattern pieces on the fusible web paper backing
and cut out all pieces. Peel the fusible web paper backing
from all pieces. Position each piece on shirt with right side of
the fabric up. Iron patterns on as directed for the fusible web.

Sew pieces on with a medium width loose zigzag stitch.

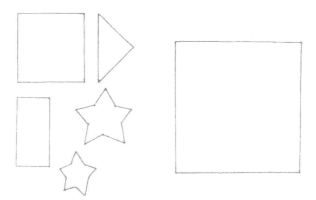

Panel Denim Shirt

Anytime is stitching time.

Print the full size applique patterns:

www.FreeApplique.com/applique.data/panel1a.gif
www.FreeApplique.com/applique.data/panel2d.gif
www.FreeApplique.com/applique.data/panel3.gif
www.FreeApplique.com/applique.data/panel4.gif
www.FreeApplique.com/applique.data/panel5.gif

Supplies:

Denim shirt
22" of fabric for panels and collar and cuffs
Thread to match
Fusible web

Panel Denim Shirt Instructions

The pattern for the panels is for a size large denim shirt. If you applique a larger shirt, you will have to add a little more all the way around the pattern.

First, pin the panels on both sides of the front of the shirt by turning under on all sides of the panel so you don't have any raw edges. Sew down with a loose zigzag stitch all the way around.

Then with fabric scraps to match the panels, you can add the hearts and stars. Iron fusible web to the fabric scraps. Follow the manufacturer's directions for ironing on the fusible web. With the panel fabric, you will make the collar and strip on the cuffs so you will have to iron the fusible web on that left over fabric too.

After you have the fusible web on the panel fabric, cut two strips 17 1/2" long by 1 1/4" wide. One strip will be for the collar and the other strip will go around the cuffs.

Trace the hearts and stars on the fabric scraps with the fusible web applied. Then cut all pieces and pull the fusible web paper backing off. Position each piece on the panels you had sewed on with right side up. Iron on pattern pieces on the panel as directed by fusible web. Sew the pattern pieces on with a medium tight zigzag.

This is a little harder to make and takes more time but it is well worth it.

Miscellaneous
Applique

MISCELLANEOUS PATTERNS

Here you'll find lots of fun ideas to add to your wardrobe and home. Horses, geometric designs, patchwork quilt patterns and flower shapes are just the start of a fun appliqué project.

Mix up the colors, prints and shapes to create memorable gift items and clothing. You can choose a theme or a color palette to get started. Then, the sky's the limit. There's no end to the combinations and ideas you'll come up with, once you get started.

Arkansas Block Shirt

Buttons and patches and the cold wind blowing
...the days pass quickly when I am sewing.

Print the full size applique patterns:
www.FreeApplique.com/applique.data/xpatt1.jpg
www.FreeApplique.com/applique.data/xpatt2.jpg

Supplies:

Denim shirt
Fabric scraps
Thread to match
Fusible web

Arkansas Block Shirt Instructions

Follow the fusible web manufacturer's iron on instructions
and iron the fusible web on the wrong side of the fabric.

From the fabric with the fusible web applied, cut two pieces
17 1/2" long by 1 1/4" wide. One will be for the collar and the
other one will be used on a long sleeve shirt on the cuffs.

Trace the pattern pieces on the fusible web paper backing
and cut out all pieces. Peel the fusible web paper backing
from all pieces. Position each piece on shirt with right side of
the fabric up. Iron pattern pieces on the shirt as directed for
the fusible web.

Sew pieces on with a medium tight zigzag stitch.

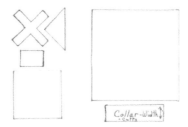

Arrow Applique Pattern

Behind every sewer is a huge pile of fabric. Use some of the fabric you've been collecting to make this sewing project.

Print the full size applique patterns:

www.FreeApplique.com/applique.data/arrow1a.jpg

http://www.freeapplique.com/applique.data/arrow2a.jpg

Supplies:

Denim shirt
Fabric scraps
Thread to match fabric
Three small buttons
Fusible web

Arrow Shirt Instructions

Follow the fusible web manufacturer's iron on instructions and iron the fusible web on the wrong side of the fabric.

From the fabric with the fusible web applied, cut a piece 17 1/2" long and 1 1/4" wide. This will be the collar piece.

Trace the pattern pieces on the fusible web paper backing and cut out all pieces. Position each piece on shirt with right side of the fabric up. Iron patterns on as directed for the fusible web.

Sew pieces on with a medium width tight zigzag stitch. Or you can vary the stitch from tight to loose on different parts of the pattern pieces.

Sew a button on the top part of the heart. Sew two buttons on the square that is on the opposite side of the shirt.

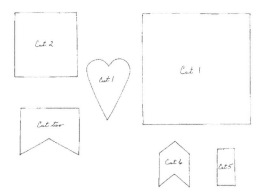

Autumn Harvest Shirt

Buttons & patches & cold wind blowing,
the days pass quickly when I'm sewing.

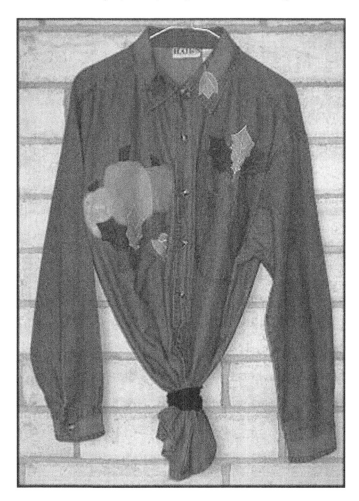

Print the full size applique patterns:

www.FreeApplique.com/applique.data/pumpkin1.gif
www.FreeApplique.com/applique.data/pumpkin2.gif

Supplies:

Fabric scraps in fall colors (Brown, tan, dark green and 3 different shades of orange)
Thread to match fabric
Fusible web

Autumn Harvest Instructions

Follow the fusible web manufacturer's iron on instructions and iron the fusible web on the wrong side of the fabric.

From the fabric with the fusible web applied, cut two pieces (out of orange) 17 1/2" long by 1 1/4" wide. One piece will be for the collar and the other one (cut in half to make 2 pieces: 8 3/4" by 1 1/4" each) will be used on the cuffs of a long sleeve shirt.

Trace the pattern pieces on the ironed on fusible web and cut out all pieces. Peel the fusible web paper backing from all pieces. Position each piece on the shirt with the right side of the fabric up. Iron the pattern pieces on the shirt as directed for the fusible web.

Sew pieces on with a medium tight zigzag stitch. When you are done sewing the pieces on, you are ready to start putting the lines on the pumpkin and the leaves. Use the same medium tight zigzag stitch for the lines.

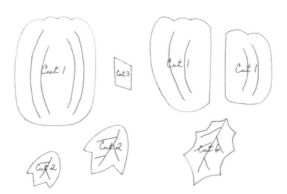

Basket Patch Shirt

Behind every sewer is a huge pile of fabric.
Make this basket patch denim shirt for the cool days ahead.

Print the full size applique patterns:
www.FreeApplique.com/applique.data/squarepat.jpg

Supplies:

Denim shirt
Fabric scraps
Thread to match
Fusible web

Basket Patch Shirt Instructions

Follow the fusible web manufacturer's iron on instructions and iron the fusible web on the wrong side of the fabric.

From the fabric with the fusible web applied, cut two pieces 17 1/2" long by 1 1/4" wide. One will be for the collar and the other one will be used on a long sleeve shirt on the cuffs.

Trace the pattern pieces on the fusible web paper backing and cut out all pieces. Peel the fusible web paper backing from all pieces. Position each piece on shirt with right side of the fabric up. Iron pattern pieces on the shirt as directed for the fusible web.

Sew pieces on with a medium tight zigzag stitch.

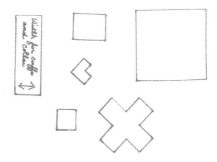

Clover T- Shirt

Anytime is stitching time....

Print the full size applique patterns:
www.FreeApplique.com/applique.data/childcloverpatt.gif

Supplies:

T-shirt
Fabric scraps
Thread to match
Fusible web

Clover T-shirt Instructions

Follow the fusible web manufacturer's iron on instructions and iron the fusible web on the wrong side of the fabric.

Trace the pattern pieces on the fusible web paper backing and cut out all pieces. Peel the fusible web paper backing from all pieces. Position each piece on the sweatshirt with right side of the fabric up. Iron pattern pieces on the sweatshirt as directed for the fusible web. Sew pieces on with a medium tight zigzag stitch.

Southwest Coyote Pattern

I cannot count my day complete
'Til needle, thread and fabric meet.

Print the full size applique patterns:
www.FreeApplique.com/Patterns/coyote1.html
www.freeapplique.com/Patterns/coyote1a.html
www.FreeApplique.com/Patterns/coyote2.html

Supplies:

Sweatshirt
Fabric scraps
Thread to match fabric
Fusible web

Southwest Coyote Sweatshirt Instructions

Follow the fusible web manufacturer's iron on instructions and iron the fusible web on the wrong side of the fabric.

Trace the pattern pieces on the fusible web paper backing and cut out all pieces. Peel the fusible web paper backing from all pieces. Position each piece on sweatshirt. Iron pattern pieces on the sweatshirt as directed for the fusible web.

Sew the pattern pieces on with a medium zigzag stitch.

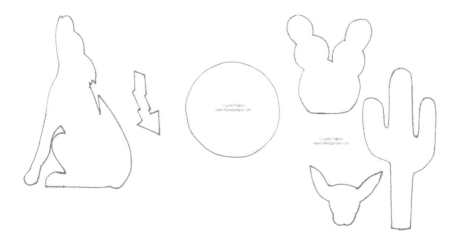

Diamonds Applique Shirt

Print the full size applique patterns:
www.FreeApplique.com/applique.data/diamonds1.jpg
www.FreeApplique.com/applique.data/diamonds2.jpg

Supplies:

Denim shirt
Fabric scraps
Thread to match
Fusible web

Diamonds Applique Shirt Instructions

Follow the fusible web manufacturer's iron on instructions
and iron the fusible web on the wrong side of the fabric.

From the fabric with the fusible web applied, cut two pieces
17 1/2" long by 1 1/4" wide. One will be for the collar and the
other one will be used on a long sleeve shirt on the cuffs.

Trace the pattern pieces on the fusible web paper backing
and cut out all pieces. Peel the fusible web paper backing
from all pieces. Position each piece on shirt with right side of
the fabric up. Iron pattern pieces on the shirt as directed for
the fusible web.

Sew pieces on with a medium tight zigzag stitch.

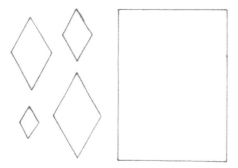

Flag T-Shirt Pattern

What better way to celebrate America than with this flag applique pattern.

Print the full size applique patterns:

www.FreeApplique.com/applique.data/flagpattern1.jpg

Supplies:

T-shirt
Fabric scraps
Thread to match fabric
Fusible web

Flag T-shirt Instructions

Follow the fusible web manufacturer's iron on instructions and iron the fusible web on the wrong side of the fabric.

Trace the pattern pieces on the fusible web paper backing and cut out all pieces. Position each piece on T-shirt with right side of the fabric up. Iron pattern pieces on as directed for the fusible web.

Sew pieces on with a medium width loose zigzag stitch.

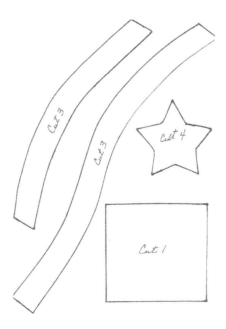

Golden Rod Shirt

I love sewing and have plenty of material witnesses.

Print the full size applique patterns:
www.FreeApplique.com/Patterns/goldenrod1.html
www.FreeApplique.com/Patterns/goldenrod3.html
www.FreeApplique.com/Patterns/goldenrod4.html

Supplies:

Denim shirt
Fabric scraps
Thread to match
Fusible web

Golden Rod Shirt Instructions

Follow the fusible web manufacturer's iron on instructions and iron the fusible web on the wrong side of the fabric.

From the fabric with the fusible web applied, cut two pieces 17 1/2" long by 1 1/4" wide. One will be for the collar and the other one will be used on a long sleeve shirt on the cuffs.

Trace the pattern pieces on the fusible web paper backing and cut out all pieces. Peel the fusible web paper backing from all pieces. Position each piece on shirt with right side of the fabric up. Iron pattern pieces on the shirt as directed for the fusible web.

Sew pieces on with a medium tight zigzag stitch.

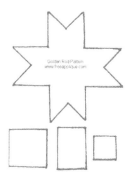

Horse Sweatshirt Pattern

As you sew, so shall you rip.

Print the full size applique patterns:
www.FreeApplique.com/Patterns/horse1.html
www.FreeApplique.com/Patterns/horse1b.html
www.FreeApplique.com/Patterns/horse2.html
www.FreeApplique.com/Patterns/horse3.html
www.FreeApplique.com/Patterns/horse4.html
www.FreeApplique.com/Patterns/horse5.html

Supplies:

Sweatshirt
Fabric scraps
Thread to match fabric
Fusible web

Horse Sweatshirt Instructions

Iron fusible web to the wrong side of the fabric. Follow the manufacturer's directions for ironing on the fusible web.

Trace the pattern pieces on the fusible web paper backing and cut out all pieces. Peel the fusible web paper backing from all pieces. Position each piece on sweatshirt. Iron pattern pieces on the sweatshirt as directed for the fusible web.

Sew the pattern pieces on with a medium zigzag stitch.

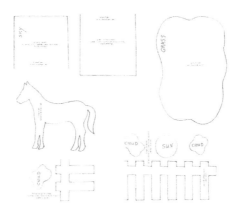

Iceberg Sweatshirt Pattern

Stitch your stress away.

Print the full size applique patterns:
www.FreeApplique.com/applique.data/lavenderpatt1.jpg
www.FreeApplique.com/applique.data/lavenderpatt2.jpg

Supplies:

Sweatshirt
Fabric scraps
Thread to match fabric
Fusible web

Iceberg Sweatshirt Instructions

Follow the fusible web manufacturer's iron on instructions
and iron the fusible web on the wrong side of the fabric.

Trace the pattern pieces on the fusible web paper backing
and cut out all pieces. Peel the fusible web paper backing
from all pieces. Position each piece on sweatshirt. Iron
pattern pieces on the sweatshirt as directed for the fusible
web.

Sew the pattern pieces on with a medium zigzag stitch.

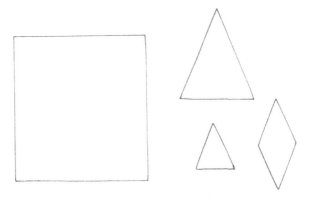

Pink and Teal Pattern

Print the full size applique patterns:
www.FreeApplique.com/applique.data/pinksspattern.jpg

Supplies:

Sweatshirt
Fabric scraps
Thread to match fabric
Fusible web
Purchased knit collar

Pink and Teal Sweatshirt Instructions

Follow the fusible web manufacturer's iron on instructions and iron the fusible web on the wrong side of the fabric.

Trace the pattern pieces on the fusible web paper backing and cut out all pieces. Peel the fusible web paper backing from all pieces. Position each piece on the sweatshirt. Iron the pattern pieces on the sweatshirt as in the directions for the fusible web.

Sew the pattern pieces on with a medium zigzag stitch.

Pinwheel Sweatshirt Pattern

When life gives you scraps, make shirts!

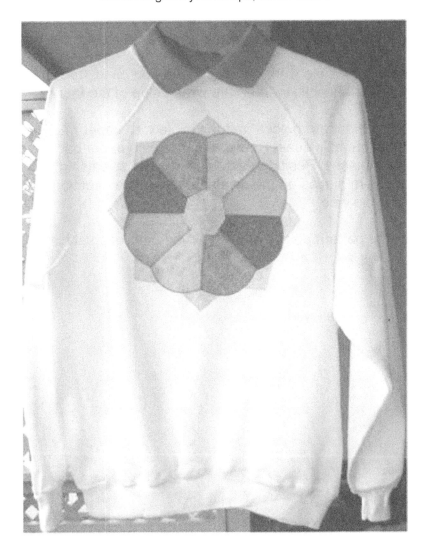

Print the full size applique patterns:
www.FreeApplique.com/applique.data/pinwheelss.gif

Supplies:

Sweatshirt
Fabric scraps
Thread to match fabric
Fusible web

Pinwheel Sweatshirt Instructions

Follow the fusible web manufacturer's iron on instructions and iron the fusible web on the wrong side of the fabric.

Trace the pattern pieces on the fusible web paper backing and cut out all pieces. Peel the fusible web paper backing from all pieces. Position each piece on sweatshirt. Iron pattern pieces on the sweatshirt as directed for the fusible web.

Sew the pattern pieces on with a medium zigzag stitch.

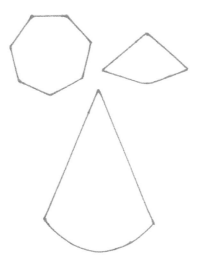

Preppie Applique Pattern

Print the full size applique patterns:
www.FreeApplique.com/applique.data/tanpattern1.jpg
www.FreeApplique.com/applique.data/tanpattern2.jpg

Supplies:

Sweatshirt
Fabric scraps
Thread to match fabric
Fusible web
Purchased knit collar

Preppie Sweatshirt Instructions

Follow the fusible web manufacturer's iron on instructions and iron the fusible web on the wrong side of the fabric.

Trace the pattern pieces on the fusible web paper backing and cut out all pieces. Peel the fusible web paper backing from all pieces. Position each piece on the sweatshirt. Iron the pattern pieces on the sweatshirt as in the directions for the fusible web.

Sew the pattern pieces on with a medium zigzag stitch.

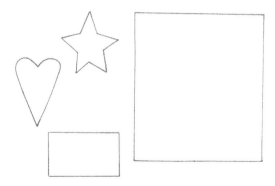

Southwestern Horse Pattern

A creative mess is better than tidy idleness.

Print the full size applique patterns:
www.FreeApplique.com/Patterns/southwesthorse1.html
www.FreeApplique.com/Patterns/southwesthorse2.html

Supplies:

Sweatshirt
Fabric scraps
Thread to match fabric
Fusible web

Southwest Sweatshirt Instructions

Follow the fusible web manufacturer's iron on instructions and iron the fusible web on the wrong side of the fabric.

Trace the pattern pieces on the fusible web paper backing and cut out all pieces. Peel the fusible web paper backing from all pieces. Position each piece on sweatshirt. Iron pattern pieces on the sweatshirt as directed for the fusible web. Sew the pattern pieces on with a medium zigzag stitch.

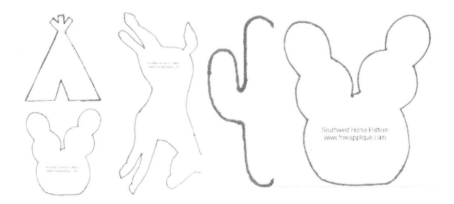

Triangle Cardigan Jacket

Never let a sewing machine know you are in a hurry....

Print the full size applique patterns:
www.FreeApplique.com/applique.data/triangle2a.gif

Supplies:

Cardigan sweatshirt
Fabric scraps
Thread to match
Fusible web

Triangle Cardigan Sweatshirt

Follow the fusible web manufacturer's iron on instructions and iron the fusible web on the wrong side of the fabric.

After doing the above, trace your pattern pieces on the fusible web and cut out all pieces. Remove fusible web paper backing from all pieces. Position each piece of sweatshirt with right side of the fabric up. Iron pattern pieces on the shirt as directed for the fusible web.

Sew pieces on with a medium tight zigzag stitch. I also added a few pieces of this design to the back of the sweatshirt.

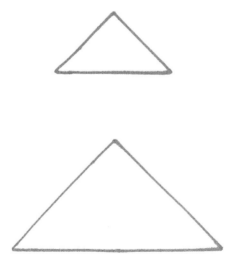

Windmill Sweatshirt Pattern

A fat quarter is not a body part!

Print the full size applique patterns:
www.FreeApplique.com/applique.data/windmill.gif

Supplies:

Sweatshirt
Fabric scraps
Thread to match fabric
Fusible web

Windmill Sweatshirt Instructions

Follow the fusible web manufacturer's iron on instructions and iron the fusible web on the wrong side of the fabric.

Trace the pattern pieces on the fusible web paper backing and cut out all pieces. Peel the fusible web paper backing from all pieces. Position each piece on sweatshirt. Iron pattern pieces on the sweatshirt as directed for the fusible web. Sew the pattern pieces on with a medium zigzag stitch.

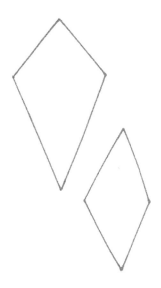

Windmill Vest Pattern

Behind every sewer is a huge pile of fabric.

Photo shows front and back of vest

Print the full size applique patterns:
www.FreeApplique.com/applique.data/triangle1.gif

Supplies:

Vest
Fabric scraps
Thread to match
Fusible web

Windmill Vest Instructions

This is a very simple design to make and fun to sew. You can put this design on any vest. I also added the design to the back as you can see in the picture.

Follow the fusible web manufacturer's iron on instructions and iron the fusible web on the wrong side of the fabric.

Trace the pattern pieces on the fusible web paper backing and cut out all pieces. Peel the fusible web paper backing from all pieces. Position each piece on shirt with right side of the fabric up. Iron pattern pieces on the vest with right side of the fabric up. Iron pattern pieces on the vest as directed for the fusible web.

Sew pieces on with a tight zigzag stitch.

CHILDREN'S PATTERNS

Kids love color, and appliqués are a quick and easy way to add punch to shirts, skirts, pants and accessories for a child's room. Teddy bears, puppies and kittens make great embellishments, and you can use any color or combination to create cute and practical items for your child to wear and enjoy.

Child's Clover Sweatshirt

Sewing and crafts fill my days....Not to mention the living room, bedroom and closet.

Print the full size applique patterns:
www.FreeApplique.com/Patterns/childcloverpat.html

Supplies:

Child's sweatshirt
Fabric scraps
Thread to match
Fusible web

Child's Clover Sweatshirt Instructions

Follow the fusible web manufacturer's iron on instructions and iron the fusible web on the wrong side of the fabric.

Trace the pattern pieces on the fusible web paper backing and cut out all pieces. Peel the fusible web paper backing from all pieces. Position each piece on sweatshirt with right side of the fabric up. Iron pattern pieces on the sweatshirt as directed for the fusible web. Sew pieces on with a medium tight zigzag stitch.

Child's Kitty Sweatshirt

Sewing mends the soul.

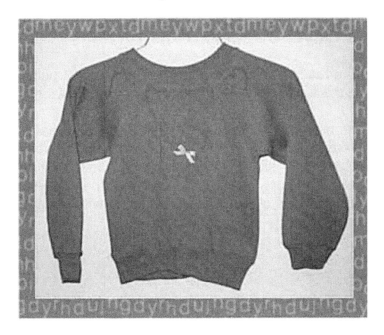

Print the full size applique patterns:
www.FreeApplique.com/Patterns/childkittypat.html

Supplies:

Child's Sweatshirt or T-Shirt
Fabric scraps
Thread to match
Fusible web
Small amount of ribbon

Child's Kitty Sweatshirt Instructions

Follow the fusible web manufacturer's iron on instructions and iron the fusible web on the wrong side of the fabric.

Trace the pattern pieces on the fusible web paper backing and cut out all pieces. Peel the fusible web paper backing from all pieces. Position each piece on sweatshirt or T-Shirt with right side of the fabric up. Iron pattern pieces on the shirt as directed for the fusible web.

Sew pieces on with a medium tight zigzag stitch.

Child's Puppy Sweatshirt

My husband lets me buy all the fabric I can hide.

Print the full size applique patterns:
www.FreeApplique.com/Patterns/childpuppypat.html

Supplies:

Child's Sweatshirt or T-Shirt
Fabric scraps
Thread to match
Fusible web
Small amount of ribbon

Child's Puppy Sweatshirt Instructions

Follow the fusible web manufacturer's iron on instructions and iron the fusible web on the wrong side of the fabric.

Trace the pattern pieces on the fusible web paper backing and cut out all pieces. Peel the fusible web paper backing from all pieces. Position each piece on sweatshirt or T-Shirt with right side of the fabric up. Iron pattern pieces on the shirt as directed for the fusible web.

Sew pieces on with a medium tight zigzag stitch.

Child's Teddy Bear Sweatshirt

May your bobbin always be full.

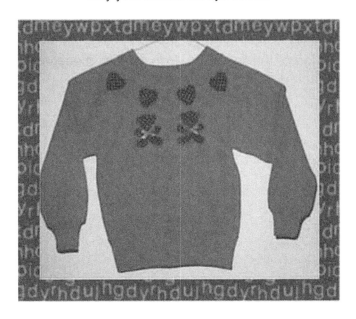

Print the full size applique patterns:
www.FreeApplique.com/Patterns/childteddybearpat.html

Supplies:

Child's Sweatshirt or T-Shirt
Fabric scraps
Thread to match
Fusible web
Small amount of ribbon

Teddy Bear Sweatshirt Instructions

Follow the fusible web manufacturer's iron on instructions and iron the fusible web on the wrong side of the fabric.

Trace the pattern pieces on the fusible web paper backing and cut out all pieces. Peel the fusible web paper backing from all pieces. Position each piece on sweatshirt or T-Shirt with right side of the fabric up. Iron pattern pieces on the shirt as directed for the fusible web. Sew pieces on with a medium tight zigzag stitch.

Photo credits:
Cover photo by Daria Karaulnik/Photos.com

Other photos and backgrounds:
Olga Telnova
Tatiananna
Crystal67
Neeley Spotts
Marina Glazova
Olga Usikova

Made in the USA
Las Vegas, NV
02 November 2024

10911392R00075